Catherina Romana Baetjer

Carteret and Bryant Genealogy

Catherina Romana Baetjer

Carteret and Bryant Genealogy

ISBN/EAN: 9783337063191

Printed in Europe, USA, Canada, Australia, Japan

Cover: Foto ©Andreas Hilbeck / pixelio.de

More available books at **www.hansebooks.com**

BY

CATHARINA ROMANA BAETJER.

New York:

DEMPSEY & CARROLL, ART STATIONERS,

46 E. 14TH ST., UNION SQUARE, (South),

1887.

PREFACE.

This little work was commenced in London, England, in the year 1871, and completed in New York in the year 1886.

The writer having spent much time, and with very careful searches and researches, decided to complete it with the one genealogical line: including some biographical sketches and incidents in the family.

LOYAL DEVOIR

Carteret Coat of Arms.

INDEX.

DESCENDANTS

Cornelius and Hannah Bryant.

Hannah Carteret, a lineal descendant of Sir George Carteret, first proprietor of the Eastern division of New Jersey, and Johannis Breijandt, one of the early Dutch settlers of Hackensack, New Jersey.

Sir George Carteret received the grant of New Ceanie, afterwards called New Jersey, from James the Second, but he did not come to America, as did Lord Berkley. He sent his son James, who proved unqualified for the position ; the life here was distasteful to him. Sir George therefore sent his fourth cousin, Philip Carteret to take charge of his interests. He arrived in the ship " Philip," in the latter part of 1666, and at once took the oath and entered upon his duties ; first residing at Amboy, New Jersey, and then made Elizabeth Towne his home.

In April, 1681, he married the widow of William Lawrence, who was the daughter of Richard Smith, of Tows Neck, L. I. She came to reside at the Carteret mansion at Elizabeth Towne, then the most prominent town in New Jersey, having been named Elizabeth after Lady Elizabeth Carteret, of the Isle of Jersey in England, after whom also the Elizabeth Castle at the Isle of Jersey was named.

Governor Philip Carteret died at Elizabeth Towne, New Jersey, in December, 1682, leaving no children. His property consisted of slaves and some real estate, which he bequeathed to his wife, with the exception of some small bequests to the parish of St. John's at St. Helier, in the Isle of Jersey ; he also desired that his remains should be placed in the vault of his friend, Peter Stuyvesant, in New York.

Elizabeth, widow of Governor Philip Carteret, married Col. Richard Townley, also an Englishman, and her son, Joseph Lawrence, married, in 1690, Mary, daughter of Col. Richard Townley—by his first wife. They had children, and many of the Long Island Lawrences owe their origin to this alliance.

Sir George Carteret gave, in 1678, all of his plantations and real estate in New Jersey to Edward, Earl of Sandwich, and others, and in 1682 Dame Elizabeth Carteret and the proprietors deeded back the land to the twelve proprietors in America; then choosing twelve others, the Duke of York executed a deed on the fourteenth of March, 1683, conferring to the twenty-four proprietors the Eastern Division of New Jersey.

There is now a society formed of the descendants of the twenty-four Lords Proprietors of New Jersey, who hold their annual meetings at Perth Amboy, New Jersey, among whom are some of the most prominent New Jersey gentlemen.

Copied from tombs of the Carterets at Westminster Abbey, London :

> Edward De Carteret, died 1677.
> Sir George Carteret, died 1679.
> Philip Carteret, son of Sir George Carteret, died 1710.
> Dame Elizabeth, wife of Sir George Carteret, died 1717.

A branch of James Carteret's descendants settled in Pennsylvania, as will be seen by tombs in Christ Church, Philadelphia.

Sir George Carteret was a favorite courtier of James the Second, he being very gallant and loyal, and had defended the Isle of Jersey against the Long Parliament. From his marriage with Lady Elizabeth there were three sons born :—Philip, James and George. Philip was killed in a naval engagement, George died young and James was sent to America by his father, but the life here did not suit him. He was gay and spent much of his time upon the water, and from this he was called Captain James Carteret. He died in America.

With Sir George Carteret the title became extinct.

In the year 1671, James Carteret married Frances Deleval, daughter of the Mayor of New York. They had children.

Elizabeth, daughter of James and Frances Carteret, went to the Isle of Jersey, the home of her ancestry, and there married a relative, Edward Carteret. By this alliance there were two daughters, Elizabeth and Hannah.

Elizabeth, daughter of James and Frances Carteret, was left a widow, and with her two daughters came to America to look after some pecuniary interests. She remained here and married Philip Pipon, Esq., of New Jersey, by whom she had children, and many of their descendants will be found in New Jersey.

Elizabeth, daughter of Elizabeth Carteret, married a Mr. Bonnel, of New Jersey, and their descendants will be found at and about Summit, New Jersey.

Hannah, daughter of Elizabeth Carteret, married Cornelius Bryant, of Hackensack, New Jersey, one of the early Dutch settlers. The first Reform Church was organized at Hackensack in 1666, built in 1696, rebuilt 1728, rebuilt again 1791.

The earliest records of Bryants or Briants appear at Hackensack, New Jersey, then called Ackensack. They are written in Dutch, and the name was originally spelled Breijandt; therefore would say that Briant would be nearer the original Dutch.

From a letter received from William Cullen Bryant, in 1876, he says : " I descended from Stephen Bryant, who settled at Duxbury, Massachusetts, in the year 1640. From him, I believe, the Massachusetts Bryants mostly descended." He mentioned that there were a number of Irish emigrants who had changed their name from O'Brien to Bryant.

Johannis Bryant came from Amsterdam, Holland, and settled at Hackensack, New Jersey, and had a family. His two sons, Simeon and Cornelius, left Hackensack in the year 1717, and built, at Springfield and Westfield, New Jersey, the two first homesteads erected there.

Simeon Bryant married and had a family, many of whom married cousins in the Bryant family, and their descendants are to be found about Passaic Valley.

Cornelius, son of Johannis Bryant, married Hannah Carteret, and their children were:

John,
Phœbe,
Benjamin,
Elizabeth,
Nancy,
Mary, who was accidently shot when a young woman.

Cornelius Bryant died in 1792. He survived his wife Hannah many years. He was drowned while out fishing upon a lake near his homestead. Many of the Bryants' family records were burned during the Revolution, in the meeting houses at Springfield and Piscataway, New Jersey.

John Bryant's Descendants.

John, son of Cornelius and Hannah Bryant, was born at Hackensack, New Jersey. He went to Albany, N. Y., and there settled and married Ellen Sparling, and their children were :.

Sarah,
Hannah,
Elizabeth,
Mary,
Ellen,
Jane,
John,
George.

Sarah, daughter of John and Ellen Bryant, married Angus McDuffie, of Albany, N. Y., who was of Scotch descent, and their children were :

John,
Henry,
Charles,
Ellen,
Catherine,
Jane,
Charlotte,
Agnes,
Roxama.

From the History of the counties of Albany and Schenectady, by Professor Howell
Tenny, John Bryant commenced the manu-
facturing of bricks—the first ever made in
Albany—in the year 1708, and continued it
for thirty-five years. This was called "Bryant's Business." Bricks were then sold by the
pound. Later two hundred men were em-
ployed, and he was considered the largest
manufacturer of bricks in the State. He
was succeeded in the business by his son-in-
law, Hon. Angus McDuffie, of Albany.

Sarah, wife of Angus McDuffie, died at
Albany, *aged eighty years.* John, son of

Angus and Sarah McDuffie, married Elizabeth, daughter of William Giffin, a native of Scotland. They had one daughter, Madge McDuffie, and one child who died in infancy.

Mary, daughter of John and Ellen Bryant, married Captain Henry H. Buckbee, of Albany, and their children were:

Helen,

Margaret,

Mary.

Hannah, daughter of John and Ellen Bryant, married Jacob Roseboom, and their children were:

Garrit,

Charles,

Mary.

Elizabeth, daughter of John and Ellen Bryant, married Jackson Bigelow, and their children were :

Sarah,

Edward.

Ellen, daughter of John and Ellen Bryant, married James Brown ; had one son, William

Brown. Mrs. Brown married the second time Captain William Ellis, a native of Scotland.

George, son of John and Ellen Bryant, married three times. Children were :

John George,
Edward,
Elizabeth,
Leah,
Sarah,
Ida,
Agnes,
Roxama.

Mr. Angus McDuffie was of Scotch descent. His death occurred at Albany, November 3d, 1845. The following, copied from leading Albany journals, will convey the appreciation of this highly respected citizen :

[*From the Albany Evening Journal.*]

" The worst apprehensions of the numerous friends of Angus McDuffie are but too painfully realized. That truly esteemable citizen expired yesterday after an illness of ten days, so severe from the commencement as almost to preclude the hope of recovery. No man among us was more generally known or universally respected than Angus McDuffie, and those who knew him best loved him most; of retiring and quiet manners, he was energetic, enterprising and active in business; in discharge of public duties, he was capable, faithful and honest, and in all his business and social relations, he lived up to Dr. Franklin's golden rule, doing as much good and as little evil as possible, his heart open as the day to melting charity, warm to every appeal of distress and suffering."

Mr. McDuffie always enjoyed, in an eminent degree, the good will and confidence of his fellow citizens. He was elected supervisor of old first ward in 1832, under circumstances evincing his great personal strength. In 1833, after a tremendous struggle against the late Mayor Gibbons, he was elected sheriff of this county. In 1840 he was ap-

pointed superintendent of the Sing Sing
State Prison ; in all these stations he ac-
quitted himself honorably. In the latter dif-
ficult position he was especially useful, indeed no man was better qualified for such
duties, for his knowledge of the modes of
governing men seemed intuitive ; his disci-
pline was strict, but not cruel ; he was kindly
stern, so that the worst natures yielded him
their obedience.

*The Argus pays the following tribute to the
memory of our departed friend :*

" We record among our obituaries to-day
the death of a much esteemed and valuable
citizen, Angus McDuffie ; he expired yesterday morning from an attack of fever. He
was formerly sheriff of this county, superintendent of the Sing Sing prison, represen-
tative in the city councils and at one time of
his life he was also tendered the nomination
of congress and senator of Albany district,
but declined such honor."

Mr. Angus McDuffie was cousin of General George McDuffie, governor and U. S. senator of South Carolina.

John McDuffie of Albany, whose mother's maiden name was Sarah Bryant, has held many public positions, embracing a period of twenty years, and during the late revolution raised, through his own volition and expense, a volunteer company of one hundred men, who were mustered in the U. S. service ; this company was the first that so volunteered and did not cost the goverment one dollar ; this was done through pure patriotic principles.

From copies taken from the leading journals, we find that Miss Madge McDuffie of Albany, daughter of Mr. John McDuffie, has rare musical talent and has become proficient in violin playing, and it is said is the owner of a genuine Cremona violin, which was held for one hundred and forty years at the convent of Maselle, in Bohemia, and is now said to be two hundred and fifty years old. Miss McDuffie has declined large offers for this violin, preferring it for her own use.

PHOEBE BRYANT'S DESCENDANTS.

Phoebe, daughter of Cornelius and Hannah Bryant, married John Barton of Elizabeth Town, N. J., and their children were :

William Bryant,
John,
Benjamin,
Eliza,
Sarah Ann,
Hannah Carteret,
Nancy,

Phoebe Barton, daughter of Cornelius and Hannah Bryant died at Elizabeth Town.

William Bryant, son of Phoebe and John Barton, was a very highly esteemed Presbyterian Minister, and stationed at Woodbridge, N. J., having charge of one church for thirty years ; he died suddenly in his study at the age of fifty-eight, in the year 1852.

He was married three times : first wife was Harriet Maria Condit of Morristown, N. J.; second wife was Harriet Butler Stanbery ;

third wife was Elizabeth Jirvis of Rome, N. Y. Rev. William Bryant Barton's children were :

Aaron Condit,
John Stanbery,
William Bryant,
Phoebe Marie,
Anna Hartley,
Adeline Rockwell,
Addie.

John, son of John and Phoebe Barton, married and his descendants settled in New Jersey.

Benjamin, son of John and Phoebe Barton, went to the far West and settled there.

Eliza, daughter of John and Phoebe Barton, married the Rev. Wm. Townley—a descendant of Sir Richard Townley—whose mother was Miss Bryant of Springfield, N. J., a descendant of Simeon Bryant. Eliza and William Townley had no children. Eliza Townley died in the West.

Nancy, daughter of Phoebe and John Barton, unmarried, died at Elizabeth, N. J.

Hannah Carteret, daughter of Phoebe and John Barton, unmarried, died at Elizabeth, N. J., at a very advanced age.

Sarah Ann, daughter of Phoebe and John Barton, married James Paulding, brother of Commodore Paulding, and their children were :

Julia,

John,

Ellen.

Julia married and settled in New Hampshire. John and Ellen married and reside in New Jersey.

Anna H., daughter of William Bryant Barton, married Joseph Mathison Millick of Woodbridge, N. J., and their children were :

Anna Barton,

Addie,

William, who died in infancy.

Anna, daughter of Joseph and Anna H. Millick, married Willett Denike ; they had one son, Willett Denike, Jr.

Addie, daughter of Joseph and Anna H.

Millick, married Wethered B. Thomas ; first child, Evinina Wethered.

NANCY BRYANT'S DESCENDANTS.

Nancy, daughter of Cornelius and Hannah Bryant, married Cornelius, son of Captain Johnathan Mulford, of New Providence N. J., settled at New Providence, and their children were :

Sarah,

Mary.

Nancy Mulford, daughter of Cornelius and Hannah Bryant, died at New Providence, aged fity-seven years.

Sarah, daughter of Cornelius and Nancy Mulford, married Stephen Day. They had one child, Mulford Day.

Sarah Day, daughter of Cornelius and Nancy Mulford, died April 7th, 1801, aged twenty years.

Mulford, son of Stephen and Sarah Day, married Sarah Brookfield and had children ; married second time, Sarah Thompson and had children. Mostly all of Mulford Day's descendants settled in New Jersey.

Mary, daughter of Cornelius and Nancy Mulford, married Elias, son of Master William Cole, of Green Brook, N. J. Their children were :

Mary,

Mulford.

Mary Cole, daughter of Cornelius and Nancy Mulford, died at Scotch Plains, N. J., May 4th, 1843, aged fifty-six years.

Mary, daughter of Elias and Mary Cole, married William, son of Isaac Crane, of New Providence, N. J., and their children were :

Huldah,

Cornelius,

Theodore,

Leri,

Thomas,

William.

The history of the early settlers of Passaic Valley introduces the family of William

Crane ; also the Mulfords, Coles and Shot-wells.

Mulford, son of Elias and Mary Cole, married Emeline, daughter of Daniel Shotwell, of Scotch Plains, and their children were :

Elias,
Daniel,
George,
Alfred,
Phoebe,
Jamima,
Mary,
Ida.

Jamima, daughter of Mulford and Emeline Cole, married George E. Morgan, of Brooklyn, N. Y., and their children were :

Mary E.,
George E.

Mary, daughter of Mulford and Emeline Cole, married John L., son of William Brower, of New York; their first child, Clarence A. Brower.

Elizabeth Bryant's Descendants.

Elizabeth, daughter of Hannah and Cornelius Bryant, was born at Springfield, New Jersey, in the year of 1768, married Johnathan Bonnell of Chatham, New Jersey, and their children were :

Johnathan,
Charlotte.

Elizabeth, widow of Johnathan Bonnell, married John Ballentine, of Edinburg, Scotland. By this marriage there was one daughter, Eliza H., born in New York, July 14th, 1799.

Elizabeth, widow of John Ballentine, married Samuel Williams, of Hackensack, New Jersey ; no children. Elizabeth, widow of Samuel Williams, died at Elizabeth Town, New Jersey, June 26th, 1845 ; interment, Mount Pleasant Cemetery.

Johnathan, son of Johnathan and Elizabeth Bonnell, married Sabina Ferris, of Greenwich, Conn., and their children were :

George,
Eliza,
Charlotte,
John,
Jane,
Gouverneur,
Pierre,
Sabina,
Susan,
William,
Lemuel.

Johnathan Bonnell died at Greenwich, Conn.

George, son of Johnathan and Sabina Bonnell, married Esther Waring ; their children were :

Sarah,
Mary,
Charles.

Eliza, daughter of Johnathan and Sabina Bonnell, married Lorenzo Tuttle, and their children were :

Chesterfield,
Sabina,

Betsey,

Ada.

John, son of Johnathan and Sabina Bonnell, married Mary Barton, and their children were :

John,

William.

Gouverneur, son of Johnathan and Sabina Bonnell, married and settled in the West ; no children.

William, died in California when a young man.

Pierre, unmarried, lived at the old homestead.

Betsey, daughter of Lorenzo and Eliza Tuttle, married G. T. Dickerson : first child, Harry L. Dickerson.

Chesterfield, son of Eliza and Lorenzo Tuttle, married Kate Curry ; second marriage, Emma Dockerty; first child, second marriage, Lulu.

Sabina, daughter of Eliza and Lorenzo Tuttle, died when a young lady.

Estelle, daughter of William and Sabina Bowen, married Richard Bullwinkle ; children :

Richard,

Edna.

Charlotte, daughter of Johnathan and Sabina Bonnell, married Edward Bowen, and their children were :

Emma,

Jennie,

Ada,

Josie,

Esther,

Mary,

Susie,

Jane and Irine, twin sisters.

Susan, daughter of Johnathan and Sabina Bonnell, married James Hatter ; no children.

Jane, daughter of Johnathan and Sabina Bonnell, married Isaac Bowen ; no children.

Sabina, daughter of Johnathan and Sabina Bonnell, married William Bowen, and their children were :

Thomas,
John,
Sabina,
Adelade,
Pierre,
William,
Estelle.

Adelade, daughter of William and Sabina Bowen, married E. B. Hoyt, of Stamford, Conn.

Emma, daughter of Charlotte and Edward Bowen, married J. Johnston ; children :

Jessie,
Lulu,
Charley,
Cora.

Ione, daughter of Charlotte and Edward Bowen, married William Kelly ; settled in California.

Ada married William Wells.

Esther, married Frank Winters ; first child, Esther.

Susie married Irving Morell ; first child, Lottie.

Charlotte, daughter of Elizabeth and first Johnathan Bonnell, married George Pattent, of New York; they had no children; Charlotte, widow of George Pattent, joined the Society of Quakers, and died at Philadelphia.

Eliza, daughter of John and Elizabeth Ballentine, married John J. Charruaud, of France, at Poughkeepsie, N. Y., in the year 1814, and their children were:

John Henry,
Pierre Eugene,
Yoe Parine,
Emma Serena,
Frances Augusta,
Ada Geraldine.

Eliza H. Ballentine Charruaud married the second time Gerlando Marsiglia, of Palermo, Sicily; was married by the Rev. Ambrose Todd, at Greenwich, Conn., September 23d, 1837, and their children were:

Gerlando Antonio.
Catherina Romana.

Eliza H., widow of Gerlando Marsiglia,

died at Newark, New Jersey, August 8th, 1856, aged 57 years; interment at Mount Pleasant Cemetery, Newark, N. J.

John Henry, son of John I. and Eliza H. Charruaud, was lost in the steamer Pacific, in February, 1856 ; he was unmarried.

Pierre Eugene, son of John I. and Eliza H. Charruaud, married Matilda J. Allen, of New York ; they had no children. Pierre Eugene Charruaud died in July, 1885, in Colorado.

Yoe Parine, daughter of John I. and Eliza H. Charruaud, married George Ahles, of Germany, and their children were :

Yoe,

Emma,

Willie,

Fannie,

Clara,

Georgianna, who died in infancy.

Evaline, who died in infancy.

Emma Serena, daughter of John I. and Eliza H. Charruaud, married John F. Lohse, of Germany, and their children were :

Fred, who died in Mexico, when a young
man.

Lizzie,

Jessie.

Frances, daughter of John I. and Eliza H.
Charruaud, married Juan Barcelo, of Spain,
and their children were :

Antonio, who died in California, when a
young man.

Elvera,

Eugenie.

Ada G., daughter of John I. and Eliza H.
Charruaud, married Horatio Leonard, of
Springfield, Mass., and their children were :

Ada Eliza,

Pierre Eugene, who died in California,
when a young man.

Ada, widow of Horatio Leonard, married
the second time, Waldamer Lund, of Copen-
hagen ; they had one child, Dena Carteret
Lund. Ada G. Lund died in California June
10th, 1884.

Gerlando Antonio, son of Gerlando and

Eliza H. Marsiglia, died at Elizabeth, N. J., aged twenty-two months; interment at Mount Pleasant Cemetery, Newark, N. J.

Catherina Romana, daughter of Gerlando and Eliza H. Marsiglia, married Francis A., son of Eyra Cleveland, of Elizabeth, New Jersey, a relative of President Grover Cleveland ; they had one child, Leonore Hermina Cleveland.

Catherina Romana Cleveland married the second time, Hermann Baetjer, of Bremen, Germany.

Willie I., son of George and Joe Ahles, married Lillian Bell ; their first child, Richard Ahles.

Joe, daughter of George and Joe Ahles, married Edward Walker ; their first child, Evaline Gurtrude Walker.

Emma, daughter of George and Joe Ahles, married John Lawrence, of Long Island.

Clara, daughter of George and Joe Ahles, married Charles Russell ; their first child, Grace Russell.

Lizzie, daughter of John F. and Emma S. Lohse, married Mr. Hall, of San Francisco.

Elvira, daughter of Juan and Frances Barcelo, married John Vanderhoof, of Brooklyn ; their first child, Harrold Vanderhoof.

Ada Eliza, daughter of Ada and Horatio Leonard, married James Wands, of Albany; their first child, Maud A. Wands.

Ada, widow of James Wands, married Colonel A. H. Wands, of California.

Maude A. Wands is very talented ; paints and models with great skill ; her poems, for one of her age, are remarkable ; she has contributed to the New York *Home Journal*, which is a continuation of the New York *Mirror*, for which her great-grandmother wrote, over sixty years ago. The following poem was published just before her eighteenth birthday :

[*For the Home Journal.*]

THE WORLD'S WAY.

I saw a rose once, withered, faded, crushed;
Its snowy petals were all bruised and torn,
Its velvet leaves, half buried in the dust,
Lay drooping in the mid-day's scorching sun;
Only a withered rose—I passed it by—
With all its loveliness and fragrance gone !

Then in humility and sudden shame
I turned and gently lifted up the flower;
And reaching home I moistened its pale leaves,
Hoping it would revive within the hour.
But silently I watched the rose and sighed,
For in the sunset's glow it drooped and died.

Oh, why, when hearts are bleeding, torn and crushed,
Tired of the world and all its petty strife,
Do we pass on unheeding with the crowd,
When one kind word might brighten some one's life ?
—MAUDE A. WANDS.

Leonore Hermina, daughter of Francis A.
and Catherina Romana Cleveland, married
William H. Nesbit, of New York ; their first
child, William Marsiglia Nesbit.

Leonore Hermina Cleveland Nesbit has musical talent, and when quite a child played in public at the request of the principal of the Freehold Young Ladies' Seminary in New Jersey, where Miss Cleveland graduated. Upon this occasion there appeared several criticisms, predicting a brilliant career, and after leaving school she was placed under the tuition of S. B. Mills, of New York, who calls her one of his best pupils.

Mrs. Nesbit is the recipient of an autograph letter from President Cleveland, expressing his admiration and appreciation of a present which he received from Mrs. Nesbit upon his birthday, March 18th, 1886—the family coat of arms, which Mrs. Nesbit embroidered upon white satin.

Edmond James Cleveland, of Hartford, Conn., has about completed the Cleveland genealogy, commenced some years since by the Rev. Dr. Taylor, of New Jersey, and it will soon be found in all principal libraries.

BIOGRAPHICAL SKETCH

OF

ELIZA H. MARSIGLIA.

Eliza H. Ballentine, only child of John and Elizabeth Ballentine, was born at New York, July fourteenth, 1799. As a young child she was considered very bright and exceedingly fond of books; consequently was educated with great care. She became master of three foreign languages, and it has often been said, spoke them like a native.

Her father, John Ballentine of Edinburgh, Scotland, was the nephew of John Ballentine, who published Robert Burns' poems. He died suddenly at New Orleans, when his daughter was only four years old; she was left to the entire care of a doting mother. Her great beauty attracted much attention, and she was considered the belle of New York when the Battery was a fashionable promenade.

She was married quite young to John J. Charruaud, a native of France. Six children were born to them, two sons and four daughters. During the early part of her married life all leisure time was spent in writing poems. They were published under the name of Elizabeth in the New York *Mirror*, then edited by N. P. Willis.

Having many family cares and sorrows, she ceased contributing to this well-known magazine, when an article appeared, dedicated to her and urging her to write again, saying that her poems were always so acceptable ; to which she responded in the following lines :

They bid me strike to song again,
   And not to let the Lyre slumber,
Why should I touch, if either strain
   Must ever be a pensive number.

When I could sing in happy hours,
   Then there was music in my song ;
My harp was strung with fragrant flowers,
   No thorns did to the wreath belong.

'Twas pleasant then to touch the string,
  When harmony tuned every wire,
For joy was gaily on the wing,
  And friendship did the song inspire.

But now quite different is the sound,
  A sigh wafts every note along,
And nought but discord heard around,
  Which mocks, indeed, the child of song.

Her mother was a lineal descendant of Sir George Carteret; her maiden name being Elizabeth Bryant. She was born just when the battle of Springfield, New Jersey, was fought, and was one of the heroic girls mentioned in the history of New Jersey.

Mrs. Eliza W. Charruaud was an attendant of Saint Matthews Episcopal Church in New York, the Rev. Dr. Shaffer being the rector, and her adviser. He presented her with an album which he dedicated, and later this book was entirely filled by reverends, and was very highly prized. Her devotion to this church will be seen by the follow-

ing lines, which were found among her manu-
scripts :

'Tis only at Saint Matthew's I can trace resource from grief,
There for a while I find a resting place and sweet relief.

To hear the pious messenger of God, with accent mild,
Offering comfort from the holy word to every needy child.

There too, church music piety doth raise, the walls resound,
And echo forth our Maker's praise from all around.

Each note falls sweetly on the ear in heavenly joy,
Like songs of angels sent to cheer and grief destroy.

> Ye, who like me, would seek solace for woe,
> With contrite spirit to Saint Matthew's go.

In the year 1837 she was married for the second time, to Gerlando Marsiglia, of Palermo, Sicily, the issue of this marriage being two children, a son and daughter. They continued to live in New York until about the year 1845, when the family removed to Newark, New Jersey, as it was deemed necessary to seek a more quiet home ; for Mrs. Marsiglia's health, particularly her nervous system, was beginning to break down.

And at Newark, surrounded by many relations and a large circle of friends, she passed the remainder of her life ; and it was there that her Christian character had full field and was appreciated ; in fact her whole life was characterized by good deeds. Under the preaching of the Rev. John Maffit she joined the Methodist Episcopal Church, the old Franklyn Street, at Newark, and as she expressed herself: " I want to worship God without pomp or ceremony."

In September, 1850, she was left a widow, after which much of her time was spent in visiting the poor and soliciting for them ; and many an aching heart was relieved, and death-bed cheered by her prayers. At her house on Kinney street the ladies' meetings connected with the church were held, and presided over by Mrs. Marsiglia.

In the year 1856 the sad tidings of the loss of the steamer " Pacific " reached her : it was indeed a severe blow, for her son, the eldest child, was on board. She bore it as only a true Christian can ; but from this shock she never recovered, and on the eighth of August, 1856, at the age of fifty-seven, passed happily away, these being her last words :—" 'Tis only a thin gauze vail that holds me from Jesus." The Rev. Dr. Vancleve, who preached the funeral sermon, said : " God has one more bright gem to deck His crown." The interment took place in the family plot at Mount Pleasant Cemetery, Newark, where a monument was erected by three of her children, and the following epitaph, composed by herself and left by her to be inscribed, fills one side of the slab :

"Thou hast left us to tears and regret,
　But we breathe not a sigh of dispair ;
Oh ! no, in grief we will never forget
　The rapture that was in thy prayers.
Hope gilds with its radiance the gloom
　That closed on thy mortal career ;
We look on the shades that environ the tomb,
　The darkness that mantels the bier, ·
And think that thy spirit has taken its flight,
　To blend in the lustre of heaven's own light."

BENJAMIN BRYANT'S DESCENDANTS.

Benjamin, son of Cornelius and Hannah Bryant, married Elizabeth Tucker, of Westfield, New Jersey, and their children were :

Aaron,
Charles,
Sarah,
Mary,
John,
Abby,
Daniel and Joseph, twin brothers.

Benjamin, son of Cornelius and Hannah Bryant, died at Springfield, New Jersey.

Aaron, son of Benjamin and Elizabeth Bryant, married Elizabeth, daughter of Isaac Sayre, of Springfield, N. J., and their children were :

Mary,
Isaac,
Hannah,
Elizabeth,
Abby, ‑

William,

Emily.

Aaron Bryant died at Springfield, N. J.

Charles, son of Benjamin and Elizabeth Bryant, married at Albany, N. Y.

Sarah, daughter of Benjamin and Elizabeth Bryant, married Vogal Crane, of New Jersey, and their children were :

Charles,

Harriet,

Job.

Mary, daughter of Benjamin and Elizabeth Bryant, married John Mott, and their children were :

Samuel,

William,

Eliza.

John, son of Benjamin and Elizabeth Bryant, married Margaret, daughter of Wilson Wade, of New Jersey, and their children were :

Harriet, who married Henry Wade.

James, who married Elizabeth Kerr.

Caroline, who married Ira Abbott.

Henrietta, who married Horace Doremus.

Margaret, who married Larue Thompson.

Sarah, who married Richard Watson.

Matilda,

John.

Abby, daughter of Benjamin and Elizabeth Bryant, married Judge Joseph Dalrymple, of Morristown, N. J., and their children were :

Vancleaf,

John,

Hudson.

Daniel, son of Benjamin and Elizabeth Bryant, married Hannah Carl, and their children were:

Abigal,

Charles,

Jane,

William,

Samuel,

James,

Emily.

Joseph, son of Benjamin and Elizabeth

Bryant, married Mary Byram, and their children were :

Benjamin.

Nicholas,

Phoebe.

Mary, daughter of Aaron and Elizabeth Bryant, married Daniel, son of Richard Kissam, a descendant of Simeon Bryant, and their children were :

Daniel,

John,

Franklin,

Annie.

Hannah, daughter of Aaron and Elizabeth Bryant, married William Kent, and their children were :

Aaron Bryant (who died young), and
Emma.

Elizabeth, daughter of Aaron and Elizabeth Bryant, married Ephram Hedden, and their children were :

Isaac,

Francis,

John,
William,
Lewis,
Hannah,
Mary,
Eugene,
Laura,
Ella.

Abby, daughter of Aaron and Elizabeth Bryant, married Louis A. Dennmann, and their children were :

Emily,
William,
Henrietta,
Ada,
Eunie.
John.

William H., son of Aaron and Elizabeth Bryant, married Harriet Clark, and their children were:

Lizzie,
Hattie,
Lillie.

Emily, daughter of Aaron and Elizabeth Bryant, married David, son of David Alling, of Newark, N. J., and their children were:

Eunice Virginia,
Isaac Adison.

Daniel, son of Daniel and Mary Kissam, married Elizabeth Drew; first child, Emma.

Franklin, son of Daniel and Mary Kissam, married Anna Van Dorn; first child, Louise.

Emma, daughter of Hannah and William Kent, married William Van Roden; first child, Mary.

Hannah, daughter of Elizabeth and Ephram Hedden, married Albert Rease, their children were:

Francis,
Isaac,
Mary,
Laura,
Ella.

Emily, daughter of Abby and Louis Denman, married Carles Carley; their children were:

William,

Henrietta,

Ada,

Eunice.

Lizzie, daughter of William H. and Harriet Bryant, married Isaac Apgan.

Hattie married Judge Smith.

Lizzie married Egbert Watson.

William H. Bryant was born at the old Bryant homestead, and has always resided in that locality, holding a number of prominent offices.

Eunice Virginia, daughter of David and Emily Alling, married Thomes L. Rolo, of Elizabeth, N. J.; first child, Guy W. Rolo.

Isaac Adison, son of David and Emily Alling, married Josie MacAuger; first child Pierre.

Phœbe, daughter of Joseph and Mary Byram Bryant, married Edward Trobridge; their children were :

Sarah,

Mary,

Nettie.

Nicholas, son of Joseph and Mary Byram Bryant, married Eunice Pierson, and their children were :

Ellen,

Carrie,

George,

Stacy.

John, son of Joseph and Abby Dalrymple, married Elizabeth Mencah.

Hudson, son of Joseph and Abby Dalrymple, married Harriet Hatfield.

Vancleaf, son of Joseph and Abby Dalrymple, married Mary Ann, daughter of Doctor Canfield, of Morristown, N. J.

Judge Vancleaf Dalrymple, Judge of the Supreme Court of New Jersey, has, like his father, held prominent and trusty positions for a space of many years.

Abby Bryant Dalrymple, mother of Judge Vancleaf Dalrymple, is now living at Morristown, N. J., and is in the ninety-fourth year of her age.

BIOGRAPHICAL SKETCH

OF

GERLANDO MARSIGLIA,

As it appeared in the N. Y. Biographical Record,
July 1886.

Gerlando Marsiglia, son of Antonio and Catharina Romana Marsiglia, was born at Palermo, Sicily, February eighteenth, 1792. His father, Antonio Marsiglia, was a native of Sicily, and his mother, Catharina Romana, was a Roman lady, belonging to an old family; the name of Roman Catharine having been handed down from generations.

At a very early age Gerlando Marsiglia showed wonderful talent for painting and sketching, and it has been said, that while at a country home in the village of Julianna, Sicily, where the family spent the summer months, he would arise, after others were asleep, and paint by the light of the moon, making his own colors from berries.

When old enough he was placed under the tuition of Signor Patania, of Palermo, who had the reputation of being the Raphael of Sicily, and who painted some altar pieces which vie with those of the old renowned masters.

While pursuing his study there entered the studio, one day, his elder brother, a priest from Naples, named Juiseppe Marsiglia, accompanied by a nobleman, who was so pleased with the talent of young Marsiglia, that upon leaving, he said "you will hear from me again." Not long after this his teacher, Sig. Patania, came to him to announce that he had been admitted into the Royal Academy of Naples ; he at once went to Naples and applied himself to study.

It was now coming time for him to exhibit his work, and on the day when the nobles visit the Academy and rewards are given, Gerlando Marsiglia received the highest medal for historical painting, and on March twenty-second, 1810, was decorated by Fernando, King of Sardinia in the kingdom of the two Sicilies.

Naples continued to be his home; and on January fifth, 1817, when the king of France was visiting the Royal Academy at Naples, he ordered that Gerlando Marsiglia should be decorated with the "*Fleur de Lis*," which was tendered him on February twentieth, 1817, authorizing him to bear the decoration, and congratulating him. The following season he went to France, and was presented at the court of Louis XVIII.

In manners he was very elegant, and generally admired by the ladies; by nature he was retiring and modest, but extremely impulsive, and very eccentric in dress, always wearing guimps and frog buttons which gave him the appearance of a military man.

Among his friends and admirers was a young American, a lover of the fine arts, and who was studying in Italy; this was a son of Robert Fulton. Marsiglia and Fulton became much attached, so that Fulton finally pursuaded Marsiglia to visit America, and they accordingly sailed together in the spring of 1824.

Upon arriving in America, Mr. Marsiglia was invited to the house of Robert Fulton upon the Hudson, where he passed much time, and by that family was introduced. It had been his intention soon to return to his native land, but receiving tidings of the death of his mother, his love for home diminished, and he became more attached to, and interested in this country ; yet not abandoning the idea of later returning to Italy.

A friend of his in this country was Major Popham, whose portrait he painted and gave it a prominent place in his gallery, which he opened in company with a gentleman by the name of Clark ; it was situated on the corner of Reade street and Broadway, in the old Lafarge building.

His collection consisted of. rare old paintings, some of which it is known he refused large sums of money for, in the full belief that they would bring more if taken to Europe. His word as to the authorship was relied upon.

In this country he speculated, but applied himself less to work, although he painted a number of historical pieces; among them was "The Landing of Columbus," "Queen Artimesia at the Tomb of Her Husband," "Count Ugolino in Prison," "Julius Cæsar and the Roman Senate," "Queen Esther before Ahasuerus," "Telemachus in the Island of Calypso" and a "Sketch of the Deluge."

While on a visit to Washington he copied the portrait of Baron De Steuben, which was painted by Stewart, of London. A fire occurred in the Rotunda of the Capitol and destroyed this portrait.

The copy painted by Marsiglia was sold to the city of New York, purchased by Mayor Woodhull, in the year 1850, and is now to be seen in the Mayor's room at City Hall, New York. The portrait of Major Popham was bought about the same time by the Cincinnati Society, of which Major Popham was president.

In the year 1837, he married a very estimable and accomplished American lady, who, although past the "Spring of Life," was still the artist's ideal of beauty: this was Mrs. Eliza H. Ballentine Charruaud, a lineal descendant of Sir George Carteret, of the Isle of Jersey, and the first proprietor of the state of New Jersey. Two children were born to them, a son and daughter. The son bore the name of his father and paternal grandfather—Gerlando Antonio. He died in infancy. The daughter was named after her maternal grandmother—Catharina Romana.

About the year 1849 Mr. Marsiglia's health began to decline, and on the eighth of September, 1850, he passed away, leaving a widow and one daughter. All rights of the Catholic church were observed and the interment took place at Calvary Cemetery. A simple monument was erected bearing the palette and brushes, with the following inscription :

> " Friends of Sicily drop a tear,
> A son of Genius sleepeth here.
> God called him to a realm so fair,
> Sorrow or death cannot enter there."

Mr. Marsiglia's collection of paintings were sold by Henry H. Leeds, December fifth, 1850, at number eight Wall street. Among them was a " Madonna and Child," considered by him to be a Carregio ; also the holy Raffaelle by Raffaelle. Mr. Marsiglia was one of the founders of the National Academy of Design in New York, took an active part to promote its interests and was an Academician.

On the eighth of November, 1825, a number of young Artists and Students established the New York Drawing Association, and soon after, on the sixteenth of January, 1826, they resolved themselves into a new organization, to be known as the National Academy of the Arts of Design. They, thereupon, chose from their number fifteen artists, who were directed to choose fifteen others—the thirty thus selected to constitute the New Society.

Of this body of Founders of the National Academy of design, whose names are here recorded, Mr. Thos. S. Cummings, N. A., who was for many years the Treasurer, and at one time the Vice-President of the Academy, is now the only survivor.

THE FIRST FIFTEEN.

CUMMINGS, THOS. S.,	MARSIGLIA, G.,
DANFORTH, M. L.,	MAVERECK, PETER,
DUNLAP, WM.,	POTTER, EDW. C.,
DURAND, A. B.,	REINAGLE, HUGH,
FRAZEE, JOHN,	TOWN, ITHIEL,
INMAN, HENRY,	WRIGHT, CHAS. C.,
INGHAM, CHAS. C.,	WALL, W. G.,
MORSE, S. F. B,	

www.ingramcontent.com/pod-product-compliance
Lightning Source LLC
Chambersburg PA
CBHW031746090426
42739CB00008B/905